Community Policing and Crime Prevention in America and England

Robert C. Wadman, *Chief of Police,*
Wilmington Police Department, Wilmington, North Carolina
and
Sir Stanley E. Bailey, *Chief Constable,*
Northumbria Police, Northumbria, England

HV
7936
.C83
W33
1993
West

Office of International Criminal Justice
University of Illinois at Chicago

Library of Congress Cataloging-in-Publication Data

Wadman, Robert C.
Community policing and crime prevention in America and England / Robert C.
Wadman and Sir Stanley E. Bailey.
p. cm.
Includes index.
ISBN 0-942511-50-6
1. Community policing—United States. 2. Community policing—Great Britain.
3. Crime prevention—United States—Citizen participation. 4. Crime prevention—Great Britain—Citizen participation. I. Bailey, Stanley E., Sir, 1926— .
II. Title. HV7936. C83W33 1993
363.2'3—dc20

92-44179
CIP

© 1993 by the Office of International Criminal Justice
Published and distributed by the Office of International Criminal Justice
The University of Illinois at Chicago
1333 South Wabash Avenue, Box 53
Chicago, Illinois 60605
and distributed by
The Office of International Criminal Justice-Europe
University of Illinois Office
Gyosei International College
London Road
Reading, Berkshire RG1 5AQ
United Kingdom

Production Design: Bernadette Oden

Acknowledgments

Captain Byron Suam
Aurora, Illinois Police Department
and
Superintendent Wilf Laidler
Chief Constable's Office
Force Headquarters,
Newcastle-upon-Tyne,
United Kingdom

Their helpful discussions refined our work.

Contents

Community Policing
and
Crime Prevention
in
America and England

1

Detection, Conviction, or Prevention?

... Crime will not be tackled effectively if it is regarded as solely a matter for the police. Effective action against crime requires the police and all sections of the community to work together in partnership.

—The Rt. Hon. Douglas Hurd, Secretary of State for Home Affairs, United Kingdom.

. . . The spectre of violent crime and the knowledge that, without warning, any person can be attacked or crippled, robbed or killed, lurks at the fringes of consciousness. Every citizen of this country is more impoverished, less free, more fearful, and less safe because of the ever-present threat of the criminal. Rather than alter a system that has proven itself incapable of dealing with crime, society has altered itself.

—President's Task Force on Victims of Crime.

Police officers know a lot about crime. Every day they see crime from the victim's point of view; they see the loss, the hurt, the suffering. What police also need to do is think about the wider effects of crime.

The fear of crime and of the reality of it undermines communities. It destroys businesses and jobs, because no one wants to establish a business in an area plagued by vandalism, violence, and drugs. Communities can try to solve these problems, but crime will hinder a community's efforts to solve problems.

Dealing with crime is enormously expensive. The cost for criminal justice services in Great Britain is well over $7 billion; the cost in the U.S. is ten times that amount.

Basic information is needed on the techniques and procedures which can be employed to prevent and reduce crime in the communities where operational police serve. Although the latest theories from criminology and sociology will not be outlined, it is hoped that this book will reexamine crime prevention in a direct and relevant way.

Levels of reported crime in both the U.S. and the United Kingdom have risen consistently since the end of World War II (Figure 1). Both countries are more prosperous, and in each there are more cars and luxury goods to steal. Because every-

U.S. Major Crimes 1943-1971
(rates per 100,000 population)

	1943	1948	1953	1958	1963	1968	1971
MURDER	5.6	6	5	4.6	4.5	6.75	8.5
RAPE	7.7	7.8	7.5	9.5	9.25	15.75	20.25
ROBBERY	48	55	57	58	61	132	185
ASSAULT	52	70	80	82	90	140	175
BURG.	260	300	350	425	575	910	1150
TOTALS

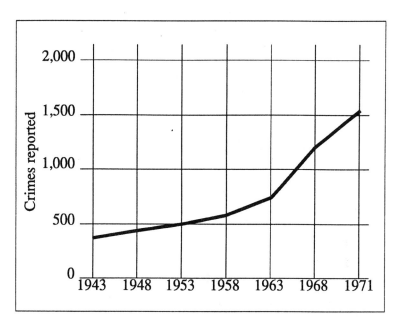

Figure 1.

Information about the extent to which crime is reported to police has only become widely available in the past decade.

It has long been known that many crimes do not come to the attention of the police, but it was only with the development of victimization surveys that systematic information became available on crimes that are not reported.

Early surveys undertaken by researchers working with the President's Commission on Law Enforcement and Administration of Justice in 1967 undertook studies to measure the so-called "dark figure" of crime. These early surveys found that a vast number of crimes do not come to police attention.

Since 1973, the National Crime Survey has provided yearly findings on the extent to which crimes are reported to the police, the characteristics of crimes that are and are not reported, and the reasons for not reporting.

Figure 2. Only a third of all crimes are reported to the police

Reporting rates varied by type of crime and sex and age of victim—but not by race

In 1981, the rate of reporting to the police was higher for violent crimes than for personal crimes of theft (47% vs. 27%), female than for male victims of violent crimes (52% vs. 44%), and older than for younger victims.

Whites, blacks, Hispanics, and non-Hispanics reported both violent crimes and personal crimes of theft at more or less the same rates.

Reporting rates were higher for motor vehicle theft than for burglary and for household larceny

In 1981, the rates of reporting to the police were
67% for motor vehicle theft,
51% for household burglary, and
26% for household larceny.

There were only minor differences in the rates at which whites and blacks reported these three household crimes.

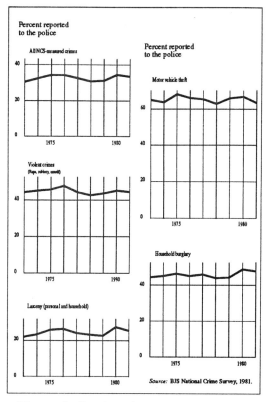

Figure 2. Continued

one pays for insurance, it is assumed that they will report thefts to the police. However, research in both countries in the 1980s indicates that only a small proportion of crime is ever reported to the police. A considerable amount of crime is never reported (Figure 2). The monetary value of unreported crime has become known as the invisible cost of crime.

According to statistics almost a total of 11 billion dollars was lost in crime in the United States in 1981. Multiplying that number by three—on the optimistic basis that a third of the offenses are reported—results in a figure of 90 million dollars lost every day.

Concerning levels of successful detection—generally around 40 percent for most police forces—police are not dealing with crime effectively.

Yet police budgets are shrinking, and the pressure on resources is always increasing. Police continue to concentrate on criminal activity with very little success.

Something is wrong. A criminal attack can leave the victim emotionally or physically shattered, perhaps for life. Yet by conventional police standards if the offense is detected and the criminal apprehended, police are considered successful.

Police need to reexamine their original aims and objectives and remember that the prime purpose of an efficient police is the prevention of crime.

One simple reason why police are emphasizing prevention is that *it works.*

It makes sense to show old people how they can protect themselves from intruders in their homes.

It makes sense to teach children to protect themselves from molestation.

More important, it makes sense to help people *to help themselves* to reduce their fear and concern about crime. A strident or sensational crime prevention campaign can increase fear and concern. Police forces, for example, can provide information and statistics about local crime in a way that is honest, informative, and reassuring.

Police officers can help the public prevent criminal behavior by understanding criminal conduct, victim behavior, and crime development. For example, some people are more likely than others to become victims.

A 1983 *U.S. Bureau of Justice Statistics Report to the Nation on Crime* identified some of the key features of the groups of people likely to be victimized. Sixteen to twenty-four year olds are five times more likely to be victimized than fifty to sixty year olds. Men are twice as likely to be victimized as women. Blacks are more likely to be victimized than whites. Levels of violent crime are more common in low income groups than in high income groups.

Similar groups of victims can be found in Great Britain.

Children of single parent families tend to disproportionately break laws. Low academic achievement is another indicator of potential criminal behavior. Clear evidence exists that a great deal of crime is committed by small groups of career criminals. One study reported that 23 percent of incarcerated offenders had committed 61 percent of the reported crime in one area.

Although this information is relevant, police must expand the ways they consider crime. They have to think of youth programs in schools or neighborhood clubs. They have to think about diverting young people away from crime. They have to find ways of redirecting young people's energy away from crime so that their energy does not find itself directed toward crime.

These changes cannot be underrated. They require a very different emphasis by law enforcement agencies, because the police officer begins to move into a position as a catalyst for community measures against crime. In becoming a catalyst, police must provide the simple truths about what is happening in their communities: what the crimes are, where the crimes occurred, and when the crime happened. The police can begin to gather the resources and the energy of the public to act against crimes. If police have problems with young people, then the schools and the education services must be involved with police. If problems with liquor and drugs exist, then police are dealing with a criminal problem as well as a health issue.

Police may wonder whether some communities have the potential within them to react to crime by preventing it. The challenges to the community are the challenges which law enforcement must meet.

2

Community Approaches to Crime Prevention

Some basic "first aid" measures can result in immediate reductions in community crime. If police are to understand crime prevention, they need to know what they are trying to prevent. They should define what crime is.

Crime does not just mean a breach of a city ordinance or an infringement of state or federal law. A definition should include a perspective that focuses on what the public perceives as a problem, not just what concerns enforcement agencies. That perspective will alter or adjust police priorities.

Police must listen to the public. They can learn a great deal by asking members of the community what *their* concerns and fears are. Police agencies may be concentrating on burglary when they should be learning that local people are being hassled by a totally different problem. Consequently, police should tailor their crime prevention measures to solve local problems. Police must also learn that there are different approaches to and various elements of crime prevention.

PRIMARY CRIME PREVENTION

Primary crime prevention is a useful way of defining what police do as line officers—enforcing the law. Historically, the original aims in 1829 of the British Metropolitan Police were the prevention and detection of crime. The first Metropolitan Police Commissioners thought that the patrolling police constable, supported by the Justice of the Peace and the criminal justice system, would be enough to deal with criminal behavior. They were correct. . .in 1829. The patrolling uniformed constable was a revolutionary but effective crime preventer. Enforcement of the law and the incapacitation of offenders are basic crime prevention measures.

SECONDARY CRIME PREVENTION

Secondary or situational crime prevention includes basic "target-hardening" ideas that make it increasingly difficult for a thief or burglar to act. It removes the opportunity or temptation for criminals to act. Locking a car, installing window locks, and post-coding property are, however, only simple beginning prevention measures. They do, however, lead to no longer thinking about crime as unavoidable and ever present.

SOCIAL CRIME PREVENTION

Social crime prevention has as its aim shifting the focus from the offense to the offender by educating, assisting, and diverting potential offenders away from criminal behavior. In a recent lecture Professor Anthony Bottoms of Cambridge University described an initiative in a central city public shopping complex in the Netherlands. It had become a fairly disorderly gathering place for young people and was producing a lot of crime and disorder. One response might have been to continue removing the kids. Another might have been to put bars and grills on all windows and remove all trees and shrubs. The management of the complex and the local police department conferred and devised another response. They established some rules, telling the kids what they could do and what they could not do. They found the kids other places with decent facilities where they could gather. Soon the kids were spending less time at the shopping complex.

What the people and police in the Netherlands learned was: give the community what it wants, not what the police want. Some American writers have called the changing emphasis upon the community "the quiet revolution in policing." Increasingly, police agencies are adopting a community-oriented style with community crime prevention as its focus.

In a housing project with a high crime rate, many inhabitants are unemployed, other people are transients, and community spirit is difficult to find. If bars are installed on everyone's windows, if steel plates are bolted to all doors, and if a very loud alarm system is in place, then everyone is safe. The problems for the police are solved, but what happens to the community's spirit? Why shouldn't the police hold a meeting of residents to learn what the project's problems are? If there are burglaries, police should discuss how they are happening and when they are happening. Residents can be helped to take sensible steps to safeguard their homes and to safeguard *everyone's* home. They can be encouraged to watch for strangers and report suspicious activity. A committee of residents can ask the landlord to fix the lights and repair elevators. Police and residents can begin to find the kids places to spend their time. Together, people can start building communities and not fortresses.

NEIGHBORHOOD WATCH PROGRAMS

Most police agencies have considerable experience with Neighborhood Watch, and most officers will be aware that its basic aims include reducing the fear of crime, reducing levels of reported crime, building community spirit, and developing good relations between the police and the public.

Beyond these basic aims, police can help to develop good practice within Neighborhood Watch groups. They can suggest appointing a chairperson to oversee organizational matters and to establish the boundaries of each particular group clearly. They can consider the number of block captains or contact persons needed to keep local people informed of crime problems, can make sure the group holds regularly scheduled meetings, and can take part in property-marking and identification measures.

A Neighborhood Watch group in name only is ineffective. Without full participation and proper support from the police, a group will disintegrate. The community and the police must keep the group viable.

Neighborhood Watch is popular with the public. People like the idea of being involved with the police in the fight against crime. However, Neighborhood Watch groups are most popular with relatively affluent white middle class people. Crime is most evident in poor neighborhoods where minorities live.

It is part of a police officer's job to get groups organized in crime-ridden areas of towns and cities. These communities can be dismissed as "problem areas," but police may forget that the people who live there are just as entitled to the best efforts by police as anyone else. If the same houses or apartments in a high crime area are being burglarized repeatedly, then basic "target-hardening" may not be enough. Sometimes a small "cocoon" Neighborhood Watch committee—much smaller in size than normal—established around these houses might be helpful. Police can encourage local people to direct their attention to a problem and help each other deal with it.

In some places Neighborhood Watch has been in place for a decade or more. For Neighborhood Watch to continue as a lasting community resource, the groups need to become involved in more than crime prevention measures. Neighborhood Watch is intended to give people "peace of mind." The stereotyped view of Neighborhood Watch is that of a group of paranoid neighbors fearful of crime and disorder. It is helpful to encourage local groups to see themselves as peacekeepers.

If the police and a poor community are not confronting the fact that the kids have nowhere to play, then police may not be able to help. However, an organized pressure group, representing the local community, may with much effort pressure the city council for funds, organize voluntary efforts to raise money, and help thereafter with the care and maintenance of whatever is purchased. Most times police could not find time to work with self-help groups. Sometimes just a suggestion from police will get people to find new resources for their neighborhoods. By giving people ownership of a problem, police are likely to find help with its solutions.

COMMUNITY CRIME REDUCTION

Some people would argue that community crime prevention and community policing only came into favor as a reaction to a more "fire brigade" style of policing. Undoubtedly in the 1960s and 1970s, dramatic changes in the style of policing were adopted on both sides of the Atlantic.

Spiralling crime rates and escalating problems with drugs and disorder were met with a reliance on more and more technology. Command and control systems were introduced, and helicopters were bought. The emphasis was on a fast response to a crime problem and then moving on to the next problem as soon as possible. What was gained with technology, however, was not an increase in the quality of police service.

Some police forces are finding it difficult to shift from technological response to quality prevention. Traditional values and ideas are hard to change, but if police do not change, decisions and options may be withdrawn as pressure for resources and cutbacks in finance affect law enforcement budgets. To fail to face up to challenges is shortsighted and destructive. People must use all their energy, enthusiasm, and commitment to make their communities better places.

It has long been appreciated in the United Kingdom and the U.S. that effective crime prevention involves action by the entire community. By engaging the whole community, the police, it is suggested, avoid their responsibility. However, crime prevention is not a specialized effort to be relegated to a small department of officers. Crime prevention needs to be a comprehensive and coordinated strategy. Some ideas being developed by English police forces represent a useful model for U.S. officers to consider.

MULTI-AGENCY CRIME PREVENTION

In 1984, the British Government established firm guidelines for its forty-three police forces on inter-agency cooperation in crime prevention. In a circular to all chiefs of police, the government stated:

> Effective crime prevention needs the active support of the community. The methods used by the police are constantly improving but police effectiveness cannot be greatly increased unless the community can be persuaded to do more for itself.

The government decided to test its philosophy by identifying five towns as testing sites, one of which was in the Northumbria area in Northeastern England. The government focussed its attention on housing projects with high crime rates as well as the larger social problems of unemployment, poor health care, and educational underachievement. A team of police, coordinated by a police manager, was formed to research in detail the crime problems of the projects and to coordinate for the housing projects city services like social services and volunteer services from the business and private sectors.

The police team concentrated on burglary, auto crime, and property damage as well as on installing locks in controlled access areas within the housing project. The members of the community and police began concentrating on self-defense intuition, better housing, landscaping, and cleaning the grounds of the housing projects. The government learned from its testing, first, that individual, isolated approaches to crime are ineffective. Secondly, police agencies have an essential role to play in effective multi-agency crime prevention. They have the knowledge, the experience, and a long term interest in successful crime prevention. Thirdly, there is no need to establish local forums with the community if they already exist. If a tenants' association or a residents' group exists, they can coordinate their efforts with police. Finally, effective crime prevention must not be based on the enthusiasm of a small number of individuals. It has to continue despite retirements, transfers, and promotions. Therefore, the coordinating structure between the police and the community must always be renewing itself.

Police may have the most effective individual Neighborhood Watch programs in a city. Each program may be trying to get action on their particular problems. Usually, however, individual Neighborhood Watch programs have problems in common. Without some coordination, individual effort is dissipated. An elaborate bureaucracy to coordinate efforts is unnecessary. However, a federation, either city-wide or within particular districts, composed of representatives from each group, could meet on an occasional basis. Neighborhood Watch programs can effect changes, but a federation of Neighborhood Watch programs can effect changes efficiently.

As police develop inter-agency crime prevention, they may extend their efforts to include working with builders, educators, and social workers to improve the quality of life in their communities. Police must avoid isolating themselves in fortresses with heavy, locked doors.

In a recent review of community policing, Mollie Weatheritt of the Police Foundation described community policing as

> a protean concept: its strengths lie in its capacity to seem many things to many people and it is an ideal as much as a method.

It is for police to transform the ideal into reality.

COMMUNITY APPROACHES
TO CRIME PREVENTION
Key Points

Design crime prevention to specific, local problems.

The three approaches to crime prevention are primary, secondary, and social.

Check list for Neighborhood Watch Programs:

Does a chairperson oversee the organization?
Are there well-defined boundaries to a neighborhood?
Are there enough block captains?
Are there regular meetings?
Are property-marking and identification used?

Variant on Neighborhood Watch Programs: the "cocoon" approach.

Multi-agency crime reduction and its effect on peace of mind are enhanced by self-defense intuition, better lighting, better housing, and improved landscaping.

3

Car Theft

Crimes involving automobile theft are not trivial offenses. More than a quarter of a million offenses were reported in Great Britain in 1986, and vehicle-related crime amounted to 31 percent of that total. Because a car is broken into every twenty-five seconds somewhere in Britain, auto theft is the fastest growing category of crime recorded.

According to the National Auto Theft Bureau (NATB), 1.4 million thefts of or from motor vehicles in the United States were recorded during 1988. A recent study, conducted to identify contributory factors towards motor vehicle theft, involved a survey of some 14,000 cases. It found that 13 percent of recovered vehicles still had keys in the ignition or involved situations where keys were freely given to a third party. Furthermore, 10 percent of the cars were towed away as a means of accomplishing the theft. Perhaps because most thefts seemed easy to commit, auto theft is increasing approximately 9 percent each year. Whether people are victims to thieves or are paying for increased car security or insurance, everyone— people, insurance companies, taxpayers, and police—pays. However, police can persuade car owners and drivers to make use of some basic information.

THEFTS OF VEHICLES

The average driver of a car in a British metropolitan area can expect to be a victim of crime once every four years. If the driver lives in a rural area and always parks in a garage, the chance of theft is once every twenty years. If the driver is an average car owner not residing or working in an urban area, the chance of theft is once every eight years. If the driver lives or works in a city and either parks overnight in a secure garage or leaves the vehicle unprotected during the day, chance of theft is once every four years.

Of the crimes that most concern the public in the United Kingdom, burglary, mugging, and sexual attacks are rated very high. Only 1 percent of respondents to the British Crime Survey in 1983 indicated that they were worried by vehicle theft. The public's lack of concern may be partially explained, because only 29 percent of motor vehicle thefts are ever reported, and only 4.7 percent of the value of stolen items is ever recovered. It follows that stealing automobiles is tremendously profitable to the thieves, and that the public is unaware of this profitable criminal business. The stolen car is often likely to be involved in a traffic accident with other innocent drivers. Many police forces invest heavily in sophisticated equipment and advanced driving techniques to pursue the reckless criminal who in a high-performance car will do anything to escape from the police. In many areas criminals will try to lure police into pursuits with their stolen, high-performance cars simply for excitement. The danger to the unsuspecting public is extreme.

THE CAR THIEF IS A MENACE

To begin, police must have an accurate and up-to-date analysis of what is happening. . .and that means *all* of the information on stolen cars. The usual data available to the police are not sufficient, because less than a third of car thefts are recorded. Police need to obtain information from local auto recovery services, operators of off-street car parking lots, and local car dealers. A careful look at all the available information will tell police a great deal about where, when, and how a car was stolen.

In a car theft, the average offenders are overwhelming male. They tend to be between ten and twenty-one years of age; the dominant age group is between fourteen and eighteen years of age. Particularly attractive targets for them are commuter parking lots in the central city and parking lots near hospitals, railway stations, and airports. The cars are at risk not only because they are parked in an isolated location but also because they are likely to be left unattended for some time. If people can learn train departure times and hospital visiting hours, the thief can also learn them. Car theft is not a seasonal crime. The long hours of darkness in the winter are just as popular with criminals as are summer evenings at twilight. However, some days of the week are more popular with thieves than others. Some criminals make their living from stealing, and Monday and Friday tend to be good days to replenish finances before or after a weekend of heavy spending.

Fewer stolen cars are on the road after 3 a.m. but before that time at night, the car thief is busy, because he can blend in with other nighttime activities. Of course the car driver is also busy and, consequently, must be aware of potential crime.

The most successful criminals are those who can put the most casual front on their activities. If they stand confidently next to a car, they are almost invariably left unchallenged. It is only the novice thief who crouches behind the side of a car to pry the lock.

The theft or unauthorized removal of vehicles is most often caused by the car owner. Most car owners are not particularly conscious of potential thefts and tend to take unnecessary risks. Many householders, for example, use their garage for anything and everything except housing a car. A polite word of advice from police can remove the car from the street to the safety of a locked garage. Even the most conscientious owners should be advised by police not to park their cars on dimly lighted streets when an attended parking lot is available blocks away. An intelligent police officer should be prepared to show some initiative. Commuters, for example, often park their cars in lots located directly adjacent to a rapid transit station and used mostly by people who park all day long. The lot is surrounded by dense vegetation and is situated in a bowl like depression in relation to the surrounding roads. It is usually overlooked by only one building and is connected to the transit station by a dingy ill-lit subway. Not surprisingly the lot very quickly becomes a haunt for car thieves who may commit four, five, and six offenses on each working day.

What can police do? Short-term surveillance operations are always popular for all kinds of crime, because they tend to get results and often result in the recovery of stolen property. However, property stolen from motor cars like computers and radios passes very quickly from the thief to a fence. Unless police are lucky and identify the fence, they are unable to do much about the stolen items.

Police have some other approaches. A leaflet or poster on parked cars will inform the public about potential danger and will ensure that property left in cars is kept to a minimum. Improved lighting is always an effective way of improving self-policing. Severely reducing the number of trees and bushes around a parking lot improves visibility from the surrounding roads. Consider the installation of closed-circuit television on a temporary or permanent basis or the employment of a parking lot attendant.

These approaches involve cooperation with others. Good crime prevention depends on everyone becoming involved, and police may be amazed at the enthusiasm and initiative that other agencies can bring to crime prevention. To effect change requires a change of emphasis by police.

There are other straightforward ways by which police can enable the public to safeguard their motor vehicles.

Taking the keys and locking the car are obvious precautions often not done, even when a car is parked outside a house on a driveway. Duplicate keys should never be hidden in the car. Whether keys are hidden in a compartment or under the floor mats, an experienced thief knows about these locations as well as the car owner.

Avoiding dark and unattended parking lots will discourage the criminal who prefers to work where he will be as anonymous as possible. Attendants can easily identify strangers in a lot, and their presence is a substantial deterrent in itself. Sometimes, however, a thief will quickly move into a parking lot to remove a distributor cap or rotor arm, thereby immobilizing a car for dismantling later.

The test drive at a car dealer's store is an integral part of selling cars. Yet time after time people allow perfect strangers to drive off in a car never to be seen again. Police should advise car salesmen to ride with potential buyers, because there can be little reason for the shopper to refuse them.

Window-etching is a proven means of permanently identifying a motor vehicle and deterring theft. It is cheap and effective, and some insurance companies will offer a discount to policyholders who adopt window-etching. The more people police can encourage, the more effective the deterrence is. Police should consider etching and other kinds of property identification for Neighborhood Watch groups, tenants' meetings, and P.T.A. forums.

Car alarms are always popular even with people who have been awakened from a dreamless sleep by a cat walking over the hood of their car. An enormous range of alarms exists to suit most vehicles and budgets. If an alarm is installed, it should always be activated whenever the vehicle is unattended.

Parking tactics help to deter crime. Applying the hand brake, leaving the vehicle in "park," and developing the habit of angling the front wheels into the curb make towing the car away difficult for a thief. Physical security can be heightened by installing locks fitted to the steering wheel or the transmission column of a car. These locks can be obtained fairly inexpensively from local car accessory stores.

Fuel cut-off devices with a master switch hidden near the driver's seat are a simple way to ensure that a criminal cannot drive the car more than a few feet. Installing such a device is simple and inexpensive, and most garages can make an installation in less than an hour.

All of these approaches help to reduce thefts. If, however, the public is unconcerned about car theft, police may have to consider additional approaches for support.

Many police forces and probation services are now establishing "Wheels Projects" that provide young people with an outlet for their interest in motor vehicles. Instead of stealing cars and driving them at high speeds, young people are provided with supervised training in car maintenance and mechanics and the opportunity of using vehicles safely. "Wheels Projects" is one example of the determination on the part of police to become involved with communities and offer positive, worthwhile *alternatives* to crime.

A final aspect of auto theft is the theft of accessories installed on the outside of the car. Extension accessories should be clearly identified with the car. They should be engraved with the car registration or license number, and easily removable items should be secured by security attachments that require a specialized tool.

An alert, intelligent police officer can deter car theft. When suspicious about a vehicle, police should not just interrogate the driver; they should *check the rest of the car.* Are the wheel trims out of place on the vehicle? Do headlights or taillights look as if they belong on the particular model being examined?

Occasionally car owners doubt the value of any way to increase vehicle security. "You can never stop the determined thief" is often said, but in the context of auto theft, it is simply misleading. Most car thieves are anything but determined; they tend to be young, casual thieves taking advantage of opportunities made available to them, often by the car owner. Most crimes of opportunity are entirely preventable, but the public does not understand the signs of potential crime. They tend to think that cars are stolen in the dead of night and are sometimes slow to recognize and act on suspicious activity. Often they will suspect a hostile young man; police, however, will be suspicious of the casual young man leaning on a fender. It is worth emphasizing again that if law enforcement agencies give Neighborhood Watch groups encouragement, they can stop crime in their communities. If a neighborhood has a problem with auto thefts or any other crimes, police must *tell the people*, simply and unsensationally, about those crimes. Police may be surprised at how much help and support they will receive.

In May 1988, the Northumbria Police in England commenced a six-month "Crack Car-Crime Campaign." They considered how the public could be made aware of the problems of auto theft and devised a series of entertaining and informative advertisements broadcasted by local radio stations.

To reinforce the campaign, police persuaded local car retailers to back the campaign by adopting its themes of crime prevention and vehicle security with their customers. Buyers were given the options and offered discounts on the installation of car alarms and other security devices. When a new car is the "pride and joy" of its owner is the best time to persuade the new owner to take care of the car.

THEFT FROM VEHICLES

The theft of property from motor vehicles is big business. A thief is simply no longer interested in small items left lying inside a car. The contents of a modern, luxury car are very expensive indeed. Attractive items for a thief certainly include radios and cassette decks, although the market at least in the United Kingdom has become saturated, and prices have fallen. Car phones are as attractive to a thief as are customized seats, special wheel trims, and added-on lights.

Again, care is needed when parking the vehicle. A thief wanting to steal from the vehicle is not particularly concerned about outward appearances—he is not going to be seen driving it—and very often getting into the car will be made in the most simple and direct way possible. Breaking the window of the average car can be achieved very easily and with surprisingly little noise. Strengthening window glass for those who *have* to leave their cars in undesirable neighborhoods is sound advice. It must be reemphasized that property is being stolen for resale. The thief is going to find it difficult and is likely to be deterred from stealing property that is properly marked by the owner. A thief will know what to steal for profit and what to leave, because it is marked; an owner must know what he can afford to lose financially and act accordingly. An extensive black market in expensive vehicle accessories exists, and these items are easily removed. Some police forces have adopted a policy of checking parked and attended vehicles to look for newly installed accessories like radios. Concentrated efforts have located cars in which ownership of the property cannot be established. Publicity within the community has deterred black market sales of these expensive accessories.

Other "first aid" measures are available to the police. Packages in view are an open invitation to a thief. They belong in the trunk. A polite word from police should help the owner to be cautious. Visible CB radios and mobile telephones are increasingly popular with the public and criminals. They are easily sold or traded for drugs, and police must realistically advise owners to install a secure area in the car for them. Licenses and registrations left in a car make it easier for a thief to use them later. All identifiable items left in a car may well enable the thief to get home before the owner.

Police should discourage the public from other habits that encourage crime. Reputable car and used car dealers are to be preferred to anonymous back street traders. Identifying the dealer can save the purchaser from later difficulties, should the real owner of the car exist. The vehicle identification number stamped on the chassis of the car should always be examined to ensure it is there and intact. Fresh paint on an older car is an obvious clue that the car may be stolen. A seller who gives a purchaser a replacement set of keys rather than the manufacturer's original keys may also be selling a stolen car.

Do police have to accept the tiresome arrest-conviction-incarceration-release-rearrest cycle of young people?

Can police redirect the energy and ingenuity of youth from the theft of other people's property? In 1983 Northumbria Police opened an Exhibition Center in the village of Whittingham in the Cheviot Hills. Staffed on a permanent basis by police personnel, the Center welcomes young people from inner city areas and gets them into the countryside. They climb, canoe, and bivouac with police officers. They ride bikes in some of the wildest and most beautiful countryside in England. The police and the young people are involved in an exciting affirmative program of community relations at their best.

CAR THEFT
Key Points

Theft of Vehicles

Take keys and lock the car.

Avoid dark and unattended parking lots.

Consider mechanical immobilization.

Never leave a car with its engine running.

Encourage supervised test drives of cars.

Consider window-etching and car alarms.

Parking tactics—apply handbrake, place car shift in "park," and angle front wheels towards the curb.

Install steering locks and fuel cut-off devices.

Theft from Vehicles

Avoid leaving packages in view.

Conceal CB radios and mobile telephones.

Never leave license, registration, or identifiable items in a car.

Use reputable car and used car dealers.

Check the identity of car sales people.

Check the Vehicle Identification Number (VIN).

4

Victims of Crime

No matter how efficiently a crime prevention program works in a community and with police, crimes will occur, because criminals exist. When crimes happen, other people are involved. They are the victims of the crime and the criminal.

Crime is a misfortune that anyone may suffer, and police need as professionals to be prepared to treat its victims with sympathy and respect and to help them to deal with their victimization. First of all, victims *do* not expect miraculous endings to their ordeals. They do expect that police will respond to their call promptly and that they will be treated with courtesy and attention. They do expect police to explain to them what is being done and to advise them as to what they may do. A surly and uncommunicative officer can make a traumatic event infinitely worse than it seems.

What have crime victims to do with crime prevention? One of the lasting effects of a criminal attack is often a fear of its repetition, whether it be burglary, a theft in the street, a sexual attack, or an attempted homicide. After an attack, the victim often retreats into a siege mentality, and the effects of the crime might become permanent. Police will want to lessen the fears of victims in order to restore communities, to prevent and reduce crime, and to enhance the quality of life.

When meeting with the victims of crime, a police officer should tell them his or her name, station, and telephone number. The officer should learn *precisely* the loss or injury suffered by the victim. The officer should tell the victim what police are going to do and should reassure the victim that information about future arrests, court dates, and results will be forthcoming from police. Victims should also know how to obtain any compensation for their victimization from courts or elsewhere. Many U.S. states offer forms of compensation for criminal attack.

Unfortunately, some victims suffer as much trauma from their involvement with the criminal justice system as from the crime against them. To reduce the stress to victims, the British Government recently published *A Victim's Charter* —a statement of the rights of the victims of crime.

In the U.S. the National Organization for Victim Assistance—NOVA—promoted a victim's bill of rights and continues to research the best ways of helping victims.

SUPPORT ORGANIZATIONS FOR VICTIMS

Voluntary organizations exist in the U.K. and the U.S. to support and assist those who suffer a criminal attack. Police should know whether these organizations exist within the victim's jurisdiction and should know how cases are referred. Generally, these organizations are operated by volunteers who are provided with some training, very often by the police. The groups have no role in providing monetary compensation; they advise and inform the victim but can also help the victim in contacts with the police and the courts.

Support organizations for victims in Great Britain are gradually becoming involved in very serious offenses involving rape and attempted murder, although some caution is necessary, because very special skills are needed to support the victim of serious crime or that victim's family.

Local law enforcement agencies and community groups can help to organize an effective response to a victim's needs. In the U.S. the National Sheriffs' Association is to merge victim assistance with Neighborhood Watch programs. The idea is to prevent crime where possible in neighborhoods and to help and offer support for victims as they recover from a crime.

Several federal laws exist in the U.S. to support victims. The Victim and Witness Protection Act of 1982 establishes procedures for the treatment of federal victims and witnesses by the F.B.I., the U.S. Attorney General's office, and other agencies. The Justice of Assistants Act of 1984 establishes a new "office for victims of crime."

The problems of victims of crime were examined by the President's Task Force in 1982, and it made recommendations to law enforcement agencies. Police departments were urged to develop and implement training programs to ensure that police officers are sensitive to the needs of victims and informed, knowledgeable, and supportive of the existing local services and programs for victims. Police departments were encouraged to establish procedures for the prompt photographing and return of property, with the prosecutor's approval, to victims. Police departments were also urged to establish procedures to ensure that victims of violent crimes are periodically informed of the status of their cases. Police officers were alerted to give a high priority to investigating witnesses' reports of threats or intimidation and to forward those reports to prosecutors.

Perhaps one matter that the Task Force could have stressed is the assistance police can provide for the victim who has to attend court as a witness. Many courts are in old cramped buildings with few facilities for the public. On busy court days nervous witnesses can find themselves confronted with a confusing mass of people including some defendants. They can be left at a loss before they get into the courtroom. Good community and police support will not allow these traumatic scenes to occur.

Victim-support organizations are becoming increasingly interested in the needs of the victim at court, and police should encourage nervous prospective witnesses to contact those organizations.

Few communities in either the U.S. or the U.K. do not have some form of Neighborhood Watch or block groups. More than ten million volunteer citizens serve in more than 25,000 organized Neighborhood Watch groups throughout the United States, and more than 40,000 groups cover an estimated 3.5 million households in Great Britain.

If no victim-support organization can be located, police officers should recall what a victim actually needs for support immediately after a crime. The victim needs someone with whom to ventilate feelings and to suggest what to do. The victim may need to get someone to make repairs at the scene of victimization or may need to be motivated to clean up the scene of the crime. Someone may be needed to reassure the victim that the environment is safe and that others are in the community to help the victim further. If necessary, professional help may be suggested.

The kinds of people who work with Neighborhood Watch groups can contribute to victim assistance. Very often all victims need is the suggestion or direction from the people in law enforcement agencies.

VICTIMS OF CRIME
Key Points

Does a victim know how to contact police?

Do police know precisely what loss or injury has been suffered?

Does the victim know exactly what police are going to do?

Has the victim been kept up-to-date with the progress of the case?

Does the victim know about relevant compensation laws?

Do victim-support groups exist in the area, and do police use them?

5

Crime and Business

Crime is bad news for business. Money spent on repairs after a burglary or vandalism decreases profits. Employees intimidated by a crime will be demoralized and indifferent. Arson destroys a business.

In every business that is closed or destroyed because of crime, it is not only the owner who suffers. Employees, their families, and the local community suffer.

In 1987 £187 million was stolen in non-domestic burglaries in England and Wales. Of that amount, only £20.2 million was recovered. A large multi-national company may well be able to absorb the loss of a million, but the loss of £1,000 could put a small company out of business.

Business is constantly affected by crime. In 1987 the Metropolitan Police worked on frauds involving nearly £5,000 at risk through commercial outlets. The cost of fraud far exceeds other types of property crime, although statistics are difficult to find. Some larger banks in Great Britain estimated between £12 and £120 million each for their annual losses through fraud. These figures are too low to be accurate.

Surprisingly police may encounter resistance in trying to convince businesses that crime prevention is worthwhile.

Safeguarding the work force is the ultimate general responsibility of employers. It includes not just employees at work but at home and on journeys to and from work.

Secretaries and receptionists are very important people to a business. They are the public face of the organization and are very often the first person whom a visitor sees. They often control the flow of strangers in and out of an office or factory. Managers should encourage receptionists to check the identification of even the most plausible visitor to an office. Receptionists and secretaries need to know from whom they can get help if they are suspicious of a visitor.

Office workers are notorious for their carelessness in looking after their own property. Factory workers, in contrast, tend to use individual lockers, which employers must constantly repair. Handbags and purses left on desks and tables should never be tolerated.

Valuable items of property like calculators and dictaphones should *never* be left in offices overnight, and large items like computer terminals and typewriters should *always* be marked with an invisible marker-pen or engraving. Identifiable items are not popular with opportunistic thieves and burglars.

Does the factory operate a shift system? Is the work force expected—particularly women—to make their way home late at night? If a business provides transportation at night, it is likely to have a happy work force.

Will employees who drive their own cars have them vandalized or stolen? Again, a business can help their employees by providing secure and well illuminated parking lots.

If a business owns its own vehicles, employees must be given strict rules about using company cars, such as *never* leave a vehicle unattended and unlocked. A clearly stated company policy is all that is needed.

Good office cleaning people are valuable to a business. They discover property left unattended. They can identify windows and doors not properly secured at the end of the working day. The wise employer encourages cleaning people to be aware of security for a business.

ROBBERY

Armed robbery no longer can be traditionally seen as an American problem. As an indication of the commercial concern over security in 1988, private firms in Great Britain spent £ 333 million on security transport, £ 41 million on glazing and grills, and just over £60 million on personal alarms and emergency communications.

When employees are regularly handling money or other valuables, they must clearly understand procedures for opening and closing the premises. They must clearly realize that if they fall into routines, they are giving a criminal the chance to take advantage of regularly repeated procedures.

Particularly when premises are being opened, at least one employee should be in a position to raise an alarm if necessary.

When premises are closed, someone should check all areas, including washrooms, to which the public might have had access.

Employees should keep a minimum amount of cash or other valuables on the premises and should always consider the use of a time-locked safe.

Employers are responsible for informing all employees of what may happen if a robbery occurs. Employees should know how to act and to be aware of the dangers posed by a highly excited young burglar who may be under the influence of drugs or alcohol. Most important, they should never try to stop a burglar.

Employees should be aware of the need to preserve the scene of a robbery or other crime pending the arrival of police. If they are in doubt, the advice is to touch nothing.

Most commercial businesses will have an alarm buzzer installed in areas where cash or valuables are handled. All staff members should know where alarms are.

Closed-circuit television is an invaluable deterrent in the prevention and detection of robberies. However, it needs to be properly maintained and used. There is nothing more frustrating for police officers than to view a tape of a robbery which is so hazy and indistinct as to be useless.

Much written and visual material is available to businesses on robbery prevention. Employers should consider staff training periods on a regular basis, after requesting suitable support from local crime prevention officers.

The design of offices can play a crucial role in the prevention of robberies. Is an office clearly visible to passers-by or other workers within the building? Are security screens installed and are they bullet-resistant or simply strengthened safety glass?

Businesses should consider their employees' typical response to an alarm-activation. Do they treat it with urgency every time, or do they ever assume that they are dealing with a false alarm? Any advice that police give to employers or their staff about reacting to alarms must be treated in the strictest confidence. A thief's sense of control over a burglary will be reduced, if he is unable to predict how staff members will react to a burglary.

SAFEGUARDING THE COMPANY

"Shrinkage" is the unaccountable depletion of the stock of a company—quite often in a shop or warehouse. It is usually attributed to thieves, burglars, shoplifters, and sometimes employees.

Police must persuade employers and company managers that security and crime prevention are part of *their* business. In most companies, security is delegated to an individual, after which everybody else forgets about it. Crime prevention can be delegated to a group of individuals, but usually other employees will forget about it. One manager may be responsible for security in warehousing; another, for administration practices; and another, for distribution. However, because no one is specifically responsible for crime prevention, no one does it.

Crime prevention should be part of the job description of every member of the business management team. It should be on the agenda of every management meeting and must always be on every manager's mind. For example, managers should screen the backgrounds of all prospective employees. They need to make periodic spot-checks of merchandise. If property is missing consistently from identifiable areas, then they should consider a stop-and-check policy. They need to look for employees concealing merchandise for removal later, and they may become suspicious of employees making numerous trips to and from their cars.

Managers also should be aware of the problems associated with employees with alcohol or drug related problems that can put financial pressure on those employees to steal. A clear company policy to support those employees should be stated.

In every case when a strong supportable suspicion exists that goods are being stolen, management should call the police. Businesses accumulate problems for themselves if they do not call police, and they should be prepared to prosecute in most cases.

ARSON

Arson is probably not fully appreciated as a large problem in either the U.K. or the U.S. In one estimate of major fires in industrial, commercial, and public buildings in the U.K., 50 percent of them can be attributed to deliberately set fires. Damage was estimated at £200 million in 1986. Although fraud is perceived as the main motivation for arson, research in the U.S. indicates that only 14 percent of arson cases are caused by fraud while vandalism accounts for 42 percent of the cases.

Arson is an appalling waste of assets, because vandalized or burglarized buildings can be restored, but an arson attack can destroy them forever.

To understand arson, research has provided some information about it. Most arsonists are male, and they are usually fourteen to sixteen years of age. No type of property is immune to arson, but schools in urban areas are particularly prone to attack. However, the problem is not restricted to buildings; each year, for example, some 40,000 road vehicles are deliberately destroyed by fire in Great Britain. Not surprisingly, arson is often associated with the abuse of alcohol and drugs.

Fire prevention should be the responsibility of one designated person with a clear understanding of the importance of arson. Surveillance is a vital aspect of arson prevention, and it can be achieved by closed-circuit television, security guards and caretakers. The most efficient arson prevention program is one that involves *all* of the staff, and management should take every opportunity to stress watchfulness.

Restricting access to a business by unauthorized persons is another priority. Doors and windows must be secured, and security around the perimeter of the business should be properly maintained. A fence with a gaping hole might just as well not be there.

Businesses sometimes provide material for arsonists to use. Combustible materials like wood, paper, and rubbish should not be stored near buildings or in the immediate vicinity of perimeter fencing. These materials should not accumulate; they should be disposed of regularly. Hazardous goods like flammable liquids and compressed gas cylinders should be locked when not in use.

A high standard of cleanliness and housekeeping should be maintained to control both combustible materials and hazardous goods.

Fire-fighting equipment and fixed fire extinguishers should be properly maintained, and staff should be trained to use them.

POSSIBILITIES

People in business have a wide range of skills and abilities to apply to crime prevention. They are experienced in management and in dealing with finance. They can formulate plans of action and communicate and evaluate initiatives. They can be very useful to police.

For more than twenty years Great Britain has had a system of crime prevention panels through which people in business, representatives from local authorities and the voluntary sector, and police are involved in crime prevention initiatives. The basic aim is to utilize people from local communities and give them the opportunity of applying their energy and ideas to improve their local communities.

Many people have suggested a formal involvement by the business sector with police agencies in formulating and implementing ideas to decrease crime. Coalitions against crime exist in many parts of the world, notably the United States and Japan.

The Northumbria Coalition against Crime was formed as a limited company with charitable status and has a managing director, company secretary, and a chief executive who supervises day-to-day operations. The first two officials are figureheads who are in senior management. Leaders of local industries donate some of their time to serve on the Coalition's board of directors. Other directors are from local business agencies and meet on a regular basis to consider policy matters.

The Coalition has produced books, leaflets, badges, television and radio commercials, and press releases aimed at heightening awareness of crime prevention. In its formative years, the main goals of the Coalition involved high-profile publicity campaigns which were sponsored by local businesses, trade unions, and local authorities.

The general message from business and industry is that benefits result from helping in the fight against crime. A better environment for employees results in more productive employees. Crime prevention efforts can cut the losses suffered from criminal activity and can directly increase the profit margins of any business.

CRIME AND BUSINESS
Key Points

Provide security for secretaries and receptionists.

Are lockers or other facilities available for storage of personal property?

Are valuable items property-coded?

Is there a need to consider making transportation available at night?

Encourage cleaners to be conscious of crime prevention.

High Risk Premises

Establish clear opening and closing procedures.

Designate a member of staff to observe these procedures and report any infractions of them.

Ensure that the premises are thoroughly inspected at the end of the day.

Communicate to staff members what they should do after a crime has occurred—in particular, no one should touch anything in the crime scene.

Do members of the staff know where alarm buttons are located?

Is closed-circuit television installed in the right locations?

Does the employer conduct staff training in crime prevention?

Are security screens installed?

Robbery

Crime prevention should be part of every manager's job description. The backgrounds of prospective employees should be screened for personal honesty; have they been bonded or entrusted with money or valuables?

Stop-and-check employees periodically.

Be aware periodically of possible thefts by employees.

Be aware of the risks of an employee with alcohol or drug problems.

In proven cases of dishonesty, call the police.

Arson

Make fire prevention the responsibility of a designated individual.

Stress the dangers of arson to all staff members.

Restrict unauthorized access.

Exercise care in the storage of combustible materials.

Develop "keep-it-clean" policies and regularly dispose of rubbish.

Flammable or explosive materials should be locked in fireproofed areas when not in use.

Ensure fire-fighting equipment is fully maintained.

6

Crime
in the Home

A home represents the single largest expenditure in its owners lives. They furnish it; they spend money on it, and they probably spend most of their time there. When a burglary occurs, homeowners are usually devastated.

A burglary in which very little damage is caused by a professional thief who has taken a television set can be traumatic. A burglary can be catastrophic when an amateur—perhaps high on alcohol or drugs—plows a trail of destruction throughout a home. In every burglary, there is a victim, and the effects of the burglary may stay with the victim forever.

Very few people do anything like enough to protect their home and its contents. According to the U.S. Department of Justice, almost half of domestic burglaries are committed without the use of force. Burglars are simply walking or climbing through unlocked doors and windows.

Police tend to handle prowler calls, burglary reports, or any other complaint about suspicious activity in a routine manner. They go to search the area, maybe talk to a few neighbors, get details needed for a report, and then leave.

Burglary is only part of the problem. Maybe the complaint is about a prowler or a suspicious noise in someone's yard, but it is also part of a larger problem: complainants and their neighbors feel insecure in their homes *and want to do something about it.*

PHYSICAL SECURITY

To prevent burglary, police need to think about how crime happens, when does crime happen, and where does crime happen (Figure 3)? The answers will depend to some extent on the type of home. There is clearly a difference between a detached, private residence in a suburb and an inner city apartment, but basic and effective steps are relevant to both.

The general public tends to think of burglary as a nighttime event. Police know better. Most burglaries (Figure 4) occur between 10:00 a.m. and 3:30 p.m. with the second favored time tending to be early evening between 5:00 p.m. and 10:00 p.m.

How should police begin considering home security? They have to give sensible advice that does not turn someone's home into a fortress.

After a burglary, police and the homeowner should walk around the outside of the house and look *away* from the house.

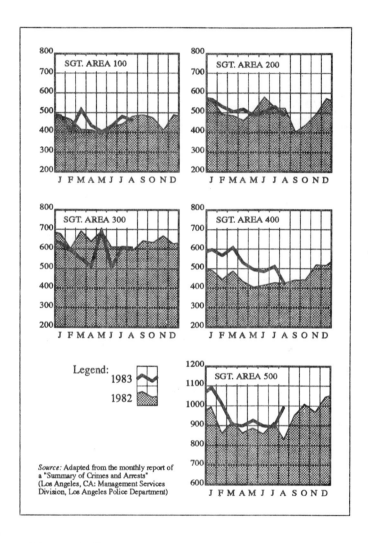

Figure 3. Selected crimes by area: burglary, robbery, auto theft, felony, and larceny.

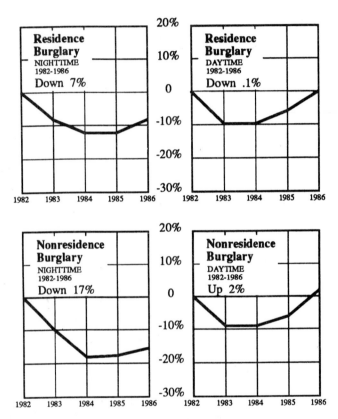

BURGLARIES OF UNKNOWN TIME OF OCCURRENCE
ARE NOT INCLUDED.

(Considering those offenses for which time of occurrence was reported,
53 percent occurred at night and 47 percent during the daytime.)

Figure 4

They should consider the type of area (inner city, suburban, industrial, commercial), the kind of street lighting, and look for any obvious obstructions around the premises. Is the property shielded by high fences or hedges? They should look at the outside features on the house and at out-buildings, garages, gutters, and cellar hatches. Does the owner keep valuable equipment outside of the main house?

An examination of the outside of a house can play a big part in preventing *or encouraging* a burglary. Police can tell people going on vacation to cancel any newspaper or milk deliveries, to ask neighbors to pick up mail or circulars, and perhaps occasionally to park a car in the driveway. If the homeowner will be absent a long time, uncut grass and an untended garden or, in winter, uncleared snow, are invitations to burglars. A few dollars to the neighborhood kids can make a house seem occupied.

Inside the house, the police and homeowner, starting from the main door, should walk systematically around the house. They should carefully examine not just the locks and bolts of the doors but the strength of their construction as well. Carefully examining all of the windows, they should concentrate on the back of the house where burglars usually tend to enter.

They should not forget the basement. People often install reasonable security on doors and windows yet ignore basement windows or cellar doors. Shrubs and flowers tend to obscure basement windows, but security is more important than attractiveness. Stout iron bars or metal grills should be installed on basement doors and windows. People often padlock cellar hatches but leave the padlock on the outside of the hatch door. An owner should make sure all locks are on the inside of the house.

A burglar, who has maybe two or three doors and a dozen or more windows to go through on the ground floor of the house, must be discouraged. Effective key-operated window-locks, available from most hardware stores, should be installed, and doors made of thin wood or glass should be secured with reinforced ornamental grills or, preferably, replaced. One-way viewers in doors and a properly used door chain are mandatory equipment, especially for the elderly or men and women living alone.

Police must consider the people who are living in the house, because advice will not be the same for a solitary, elderly woman and for a young family. For someone who will be alone, particularly in the evenings, police need to be thinking carefully about the worries that unexpected callers can cause and consider with the occupant door chains, one-way viewers in doors, and porch lighting.

The occupant should stay with the police officer during the entire survey. Some of the property in the house may be valuable and may require special security. Police advice must be reasonable and take into account costs. It may be better that the occupant does something inexpensively about security than assume exorbitant costs to deter every action.

People accumulate a great deal of property during their lives, yet when a burglary occurs they are hard-pressed to provide police with the types or with the serial numbers of basic domestic appliances. Police should encourage homeowners to do an inventory of their valuable property and keep it safe for future reference.

It is not part of police business to act as an agent for an insurance company, although personal protection *and* peace of mind are police concerns. However, police could quickly mention the need to maintain insurance coverage.

When police are asked for advice about apartment security, the officer and the occupant should make a survey of the apartment together. They should look for a fire escape. If the flat is on the ground floor, window security is going to be very important.

If the apartment is not on the ground floor, then the crucial security point is the main door into the apartment. The strength of that door and its frame is crucial. The occupant should be encouraged to replace a thin door and to install hinge bolts to prevent a burglar from prying the door off its hinges.

If a building is not fitted with a telephone-entry system at the front door, police could encourage the tenants or their association to ask the landlord to have one installed. If a telephone entry system exists, then the tenants *must* make sure it is not misused. Tenants must not "buzz-open" the front door for strangers. They must positively identify any caller they admit into the building; all other callers are not admitted. Tenants should be encouraged to report suspicious activity of any kind to the police.

Concentrating on one apartment in a block which may contain many similar apartments is time-consuming for police who should consider improving security in the whole building and similar buildings.

ALARMS

Police will almost certainly be asked by people who have either suffered a burglary or are trying to avoid one, whether it is worthwhile to install an alarm. Police should limit themselves to basic, understandable advice; in case of doubt, they should get specialists to help.

Initially, the householder must choose between two alarm systems. A "bells-only" system deters the unauthorized access to a building by the activation by a bell, siren, or sometimes a flashing light. It relies on passers-by or neighbors to act and does not in itself convey any message to the police. Burglars do not like to be the center of attention, and an efficiently maintained "bells-only" system is a significant deterrent.

The householder should be encouraged to get two or three quotes from reputable companies *before* purchasing an alarm system. A system should have some form of cut-off switch to disconnect the audible warning after a reasonable period of time. The householder should be warned by police about the purchase of inexpensive do-it-yourself kits which may offer very little real protection. The problem with "bells-only" systems is that they are becoming so commonplace and *so unreliable* that they are usually ignored when they are activated.

A second type of alarm for the homeowner is a remote signalling system. This system with a direct line to a police station is not as common in the United Kingdom as it is in the U.S. However, some alarm companies in both countries operate central stations which are widely accepted as the most secure and cost-effective ways of handling alarm activations. When an alarm is activated, the central station will notify the police as to the location of the premises and may well send their own personnel to the scene.

One difficulty with remote signalling systems is balancing the needs of the police against the needs of the homeowner. The homeowner wants the alarm to activate immediately to get the burglar out of the house; the police want to get to the house to arrest the burglar.

In some buildings activation of alarms has been delayed five or ten minutes to give responding police officers a chance to make an arrest. However, police must check their own departmental policy or city ordinance, before recommending delayed activation of an alarm system. An alarm system that is not maintained will not continue to operate, and purchasers should consider the value of an installation and maintenance agreement. However, any alarm that is ignored might as well not be installed. Alarms are often ignored, because they can ring for hours. A reputable alarm company will normally install a cut-off mechanism to stop the activation in perhaps twenty minutes. Some police force policies insist on cut-off mechanisms.

LIGHTING AGAINST CRIME

One of the most basic and effective ways to prevent crime in a home is using lights to create signs of occupancy. One or two lights turned on in interior rooms are a very effective short-term deterrent. For long-term absences from the home, homeowners should consider the purchase of timer-switches.

Police can give some simple yet very useful advice, because these switches are much misunderstood. These timing switches can be installed to turn on any electrical appliance at predetermined times of the day or night. Because the intention is to create signs of occupancy, many areas for their use exist in a home. They can be set to turn on radios or television sets, and when used effectively, they can create the impression of a normal evening's domestic routine. Police can suggest, for example, that a living room light and radio might be activated in the early evening, an upstairs bedroom light turned on in the late evening as the downstairs goes dark, followed by the upstairs light going out. Although no one is in the house, an impression is created outside of the house of people retiring for the night.

A burglar will always prefer to work where there is little chance of being detected—commonly at the back of a house. A simple exterior light to illuminate the back premises creates an atmosphere which is uncomfortable for the burglar. Another very effective deterrent is the movement of heat detector lights which operate on an infra-red system and are activated when body heat comes within a pre-set distance of the unit. The psychological shock of a sudden burst of light on a prospective burglar should not be underrated.

The security of a home is often affected by the conditions around the home. If street lighting is in poor condition or trees and shrubs are obliterating it, then police may suggest a telephone call to a local municipal department that manages street lights and tree-pruning.

LOCKS AND CONSTRUCTION

Everyone should have a door-chain installed on the main door of a house or apartment. No one is safe from unidentified callers, and a chain insures that no one gets into a house who doesn't belong there. It is important that the door-chain be installed correctly, but once it is installed, it should always be used.

The main door should also be fitted with an automatic deadlock which can be opened from the inside without a key, except when it is locked from the exterior. The deadlock should be supplemented by an amortise deadlock which can only be opened with a key. An intruder who breaks a window and reaches through to the back of the door can still not open the door with the amortise deadlock.

That most burglaries are committed at the rear of the house should most concern police and homeowners. On back doors leading to garages, yards, and gardens, bolts should be installed at the top and bottom of doors. When the bolt is in a closed position, it should be at least one inch into the recess.

Police and a homeowner should carefully examine any padlocks or devices installed on the outsides of doors. Will a saw cut the padlock, or is it of the closed shackle variety? Are security devices secured with small screws that can easily be removed?

Patio doors have always been popular in the U.S. and are becoming increasingly so in Great Britain. Without careful attention they can be an open invitation to the burglar. All patio doors should be fitted with extra locks.

The best way to secure ground floor and all other windows is stout protection bars. Although bars may be suitable for a secluded window in a warehouse, very few people would care to have them installed on their homes. Fortunately, decorative and practical alternatives exist. A number of firms are now producing ornamental grills suitable for installation on windows that offer a fairly high standard of security. They also prevent children from accidentally falling through open windows.

Armored or strengthened glass is inappropriate in a domestic setting. However, a careful examination of the design of windows is always worthwhile. Louvre or slat windows can be easily removed from their frames, but a suitably strong adhesive like epoxy resin can be applied to secure them.

Electronic garage door openers are popular but dangerous for busy owners. Having driven their car out of a garage to run an errand, many people just leave the garage door open. A lot of women, however, who have to work evenings and return home in darkness, are justifiably concerned about garaging their car. The garage lights should always be left on by the proper use of remote control devices when leaving and entering the garage. Like most technology, electronic garage door openers are only as effective as the person using them, and police have to stress that the operator of safety devices must not become forgetful.

The best door locks in the world are of no use whatever if the householder is going to leave keys under the welcome mat, on top of the door frame, or in the mail box. If an owner uses these places, the burglar knows them as well.

CRIME IN THE HOME
Key Points

Avoid signs of an unoccupied home, like accumulated mail and newspapers.

Arrange for neighbors, in cases of extended absence, to cut grass and shovel snow.

Install effective key-operated window locks.

Discourage the use of glass or thin-panelled doors or suggest reinforcing them.

Install door-viewers and chains.

Be aware of the value and quantity of property most people accumulate, and encourage the use of inventories.

Look carefully at fire escapes, and consider their effect on window security.

Evaluate the construction and security of entrance doors.

Make sure that general entrance systems to apartment buildings are properly maintained and used.

Make sure that householders obtain more than one quotation when buying an alarm, and emphasize that a good system incorporates a cut-off switch and cannot be made with an inexpensive kit.

Encourage the proper and imaginative use of timer-devices in lighting a home.

Examine the house and the back of the property for lighting needs.

Suggest the installation of bars or reinforced grills on ground-floor windows.

Examine louvre or slat-windows and consider ways of securing them.

Suggest remote-controlled garage-door systems.

Strongly discourage people from leaving keys outside a house.

7

Drug Abuse

In a survey of prison inmates, 21 percent of all murderers and 22 percent of all rapists were under the influence of drugs at the time of their crimes. However, during property offenses, between 35 percent and 38 percent of offenders were using drugs. Not surprisingly, alcohol is pervasive in approximately 60 percent of assault cases. Heroin, marijuana, cocaine, and crack also contribute to criminal scenes. Drug abuse is also involved in child runaway cases and adolescent prostitution.

Drugs influence the whole criminal scene. Burglaries are committed and cars are stolen to buy drugs and to get ready to commit another crime. The magnitude of drug use destroys families and has ruined whole areas of some cities. The problem appears to be overwhelming. How can the average patrol officer ever hope to effect change?

No one expects police to challenge the Columbian drug barons or raid crack factories. Drugs, however, are not just one enormous problem. Drugs are involved in a million small problems, and in small ways and efforts police can make a difference.

Strong supportive families, strong schools, and strong social institutions are not likely to suffer problems with drug abuse. Drugs are no longer the province of the well-to-do, but they have overwhelmed the lower income groups in society.

FACTS AND FIGURES

The cost of U.S. drug abuse was estimated by the Research Triangle Institute at $59.7 billion in 1983. Additionally, it costs the nation lost productivity. It increases money spent on the criminal justice system and private security industries. Expenditures on social welfare and health care escalate.

The total cost covers all types of drug abuse, but the cost of alcohol abuse is staggering. Traffic accidents involving drunk-driving cost $30.2 billion in 1983—a figure that has increased annually.

The drug problems are not solved when the offenders are incarcerated. Research on prison inmates indicates that before their arrest, half of them had consumed an ounce or more of alcohol everyday—three times as much as the average person. The typical inmate profile includes previous drinking sessions of eight cans of beer or more at a time or nearly nine ounces of 80 proof liquor.

"Junkies" are supposedly engaged in crime to support their habits, but much academic evidence suggests that involvement in crimes predates involvement with drugs. Most criminals seem to be involved with crime prior to their heroin addiction, with traditionally earned wages supporting a drug habit in its early stages.

Advice or information about drugs is no sooner issued than it is out-of-date. As soon as "Angel Dust" was popular, cocaine and crack replaced it in popularity. Already a designer drug like "Ecstasy" is no longer fashionable.

DETECT OR PREVENT

Traditional approaches to the prevention and reduction of drug abuse, based on interdiction of supply, have had marginal effects.

The drug trade on the street is not static; it is fairly fluid and is composed of many small, drug distributors. Consequently, identifying and observing drug trading is very difficult.

Multiple jurisdictions within law enforcement agencies towards the drug problem undoubtedly hinder effectiveness to some extent. However, the overall coordination provided by agencies like the U.S. Drug Enforcement Administration should not be underestimated.

Enforcement strategies involve many expensive resources. A considerable need for high quality intelligence and comprehensive surveillance exists as police budgets are increasingly being limited.

A WAY FORWARD

Without drug users, a market for drugs would not exist. Drug users provide the profits and the encouragement to people who want to sell drugs. Although no one underestimates the awesome size of trafficking, reducing the demand for drugs offers the only realistic long-term solution to the problems of drugs. Although police officers are not trained to counsel and rehabilitate drug addicts, the problem of drugs does not exist in a vacuum. Drug abuse happens at home, at school, and at work. Police need to think about people in these environments. They are children, parents, school teachers, and employers, and employees. To reach these people, police need to engender community action against drugs.

Police should not instigate wide-ranging crime prevention measures in the community. They should easily recognize problems with drugs and encourage these people to find solutions. Police must be aware that they will happen upon situations in which drugs play a part. A shoplifting case, a child missing from home, or a simple domestic dispute may involve drugs. Although police can recognize the signs of drug abuse because of training and experience, the average parent or teacher may not recognize the probability of drug use.

At teachers' meetings, P.T.A. meetings, and business meetings, police should discuss the symptoms and effects typically associated with drug abuse. Those symptoms include drowsiness, constrictions in the pupils of eyes, slurred speech and disorientation, loss of appetite, insomnia, and poor perceptions of time and distance,

Police should also say to parents, teachers, and employees that other factors may cause these same symptoms. Hasty judgments should be avoided, and if in doubt, people should seek qualified medical assistance.

Drug abuse also changes the behavior of the drug user. Observers should be alerted to possible drug abuse by poor attendance at work or school, poor performance at work or school, poor physical appearance and personal hygiene, unusual efforts to conceal needle marks, and stealing items to raise money to buy drugs.

Police and their audience should be asking: Where is this problem being caused, and when is it being caused? Are the drugs being bought at school or work or from associates not at school or work? Police may need to refer their audience to local youth bureaus or to local health or education authorities.

Realistically there will be few occasions when police will have the time or ability to deal with drug abuse. Police fail their communities, however, if they do not identify and refer drug abuse problems to community agencies and associations.

The problems of drug abuse in one town may be different from the problems of another, and some large cities undoubtedly have very widespread drug problems. Police should know the needs and characteristics of their towns or cities.

What may be of some benefit is to examine some general issues discussed in the National Drug Control Strategy, presented to the U.S. Congress in January 1990.

Working with communities and fostering positive attitudes in young people are relevant to drug control. A police officer, however, may not be the best person to replace a teacher in a class to teach children about drug abuse.

Police should ask themselves whether the schools in their jurisdiction have an effective drug prevention program. Since 1989, legislation has existed in the U.S. requiring all schools, colleges, and universities to implement such programs. The police are one resource for such programs along with teachers, health workers, and others.

Police *may* be able to bring teachers, health workers, and police together. Many schools have drug education committees composed of students, staff, and members of outside agencies.

Police officers can provide these committees with invaluable support.

Schools are hard-pressed for money and resources, and although much can be done through sponsorship and voluntary support, sometimes money is needed. Police should refer these schools to the National Drug Control Strategy which lists some state and local grants available for assistance. In many ways schools, cooperating with other agencies in the communities, can be the focus for local anti-drug campaigns. The National Drug Control Strategy states:

> Neighborhoods infested with drugs and crime are a standing challenge to school anti-drugs programs, no matter how well conceived they might be. Federal policy, therefore is geared not just to helping schools develop sound anti-drug curricula and form no-drug policies but also to galvanizing surrounding communities to work with the schools.

A COMMUNITY PROGRAM

Although the general public views the problems of drug abuse very seriously, people in many middle class areas tend to regard drug abuse as an inner city issue of no great relevance to them. They may be right about *their* local schools and *their* local kids. However, if they and police wait until drug warfare begins in their streets, if they wait until homicide and robbery levels increase beyond control, then they have waited too long. The time to educate and mobilize all communities against drugs is before the drugs arrive.

Police must stress the need to bring local solutions to local drug problems. Communities should be urged to bring people together to form broadly based task forces, composed of health care workers, social services workers, and the police.

Accurate information is important. Police know that some children are more at risk than others; children of addicts and alcoholics, school and college drop-outs, and abused children are particularly prone to drug abuse. These youths and *all children* need alternatives. Children in many neighborhoods become involved with drugs for want of any worthwhile alternatives. Police should encourage Neighborhood Watch groups to make use of the resources already in their community.

Any recreational programs will provide a helpful alternative. Young people relate well to role models, and local celebrities should be asked to participate in recreational programs. Teenagers themselves are often seen as role models by younger children. They can exert enormous positive influence and should be involved. An interesting program entitled, "Communities in Schools," refers delinquent and drug-associated young people to local support agencies. The young people are not removed from school for guidance; the agencies come to the school.

Once a program is given a name and a purpose, many children will be interested in it. The "Just Say No" campaign established peer-groups composed of children between seven and twelve years of age. They look at the serious side and the harmful effects of drugs on themselves and their families, but they have fun by learning how to make creative use of their leisure time.

DRUGS AND EMPLOYEES

Employers who have employees with alcohol or drug problems also have a productivity problem and therefore a loss-of-profit problem. Although some professions are more likely than others to engender stress and therefore alcohol or drug dependency, the reasonable and reasoning employer knows the stress in his profession but nevertheless cannot ignore drug abuse.

Many companies have declared policies of support for employees seeking assistance with their addiction problems. These policies make good financial sense. No company wants to lose good staff members unnecessarily. However, employers must make it clear that the person who has acquired a dependency must initiate action. The employee must recognize his or her drug abuse and determine what they will do about it.

Businesses also need to determine whether they are the source of drugs. When police are asked to help a business with drug problems, police should survey factories and offices for easily accessible solvents and adhesives in yards and compounds and initiate security measures for mainstream pharmaceutical products.

Pharmacies and drug stores are likely to be burglarized because of the nature of their stock. Police should make sure that their crime prevention and security measures are all they should be.

Not everything police deal with is drug-related. Not everything police deal with can be helped by advice or support from police or from other agencies. The public expects police to try. However, police should not analyze or overly involve themselves with the problems of drugs to the detriment of their other duties. In particular, they must not be tempted to bend or ignore the law as it relates to alcohol and drug abuse. It is foolish to think that people with problems are always going to be prepared to voluntarily resolve them.

DRUG ABUSE
Key Points

Remember the problem-solving approach, and ask:

What is the problem?

What is the real problem?

Are police dealing with a situation that they can handle?

Are police dealing with a situation that should be referred to someone else?

Symptoms of individual drug abuse may be:

drowsiness,

constriction in the pupils of the eyes,

slurred speech and disorientation,

loss of appetite,

insomnia, and

poor perceptions of time and distance.

Behavioral symptoms of drug abuse may be:

poor attendance at work or school,

poor performance at work or school,

poor physical appearance and personal hygiene,

unusual efforts to conceal needle marks, and

stealing items to raise money to buy drugs.

8

Providing Safety
from Abuse
for Women and Children

Research by the U.S. Department of Justice reveals that young people are considerably more likely than the elderly to be victims of crime. In offenses involving theft, youths between twelve and eighteen years of age will typically suffer one hundred eight criminal attacks per 1,000 persons in comparison to people to people sixty-five years old and older who will suffer nineteen attacks per 1,000 persons. Women are sometimes considered to be more vulnerable to crime than men. Statistically, men are more likely to be subjected to crime than women. Black males and females are almost equally likely to be victims of crime. The fear of crime, as seen by people in communities, seems greatest among women and especially women with children. Attacks on children and child abuse are evident in many communities. In the U.S. and Great Britain television reports are broadcasted almost weekly about horrific, deliberate cruelty, neglect, and sickening sexual assaults on young people. Also broadcasted are stories of attacks on women, involving abduction, rape, and, in some cases, murder.

Line officers are usually called to the scenes of these attacks upon women and children. However, it is in the interest of the community that police try to prevent these attacks from occurring. Safety for women and children must be confronted regularly, as police must ask themselves: What is the problem here? What are the components of this problem? What caused it? What must be done to resolve it? Cases of attacks upon women or children are complicated, and sometimes police can only refer a case elsewhere. However, if a case is referred to another agency, police must make sure it is not lost in someone else's files.

For children, many agencies are available, including state child protection agencies, Roman Catholic social services, city hospital resources, abuse counselling programs, and city social service programs. Sometimes, police need to know who is available in an agency. Many departments issue local resource memorandum cards to police. If a police department does not have them, it should consider issuing them. Often, however, police can only suggest where a troubled individual can get help. Police can, however, take simple straightforward steps to prevent crimes against children and their possessions. In suburban residential areas in early evening, sidewalks and lawns are often littered with skateboards, pedal cars, and bicycles that have been abandoned while children watch television. In neighborhood shopping centers, expensive bicycles are left outside the doors of the markets while their owners shop. Police should take a minute to tell children that if they don't look after their property, then they can lose it, especially after an assault by a thief. Do their parents know where they are? Children are adventurous, outgoing, and often mischievous, but police can keep crime away from them with some simple reminders.

A CODE FOR CHILDREN

The field of child abuse is a specialized one. Much medical, psychological, and sociological research has been done recently. However, in some ways child abuse can be a minefield for police officers who innocently try to indoctrinate children to all the dangers that adults can represent. Parents tend to educated their children in terms of "Stranger-Danger." Children are told to be wary of strangers offering candy or car rides. They are taught not to talk to strangers but not to be rude or impolite. They are told to just walk away from strange situations, and if in doubt, run away, shout, or do whatever they need do to get away from danger. "Stranger-Danger" is entirely valid *as far as it goes*. Unfortunately, a substantial proportion of those convicted of child molestation are people whom the child knows. Members of the family, baby-sitters, and neighbors may be potential abusers.

No one, however, wants children living in permanent fear of being abducted or molested by people they know. Two constructive approaches seem to help prevent child abuse. First, each and every child is entitled to personal respect both from his peers and from adults. They are entitled to expect that others will respect their privacy, and no one has a right to take that privacy away from them. Second, children who are accustomed to friendly and positive contact with law enforcement agencies will be prepared to help police and themselves, if and when abuse may happen. However, police must be very careful when confronted with possible abuse cases. They should almost always involve other agencies for advice and assistance. Parents and their children need to know that police must, without sensationalism or unnecessary drama, describe child abuse as an occasional act. Police must never portray adults as threats to children. Instead, police should encourage children to seek help when necessary from teachers, doctors, or the police themselves. "Kidscape" is an approach developed by health experts in Great Britain to educate children about abuse. A very similar approach has been adopted in the United States. Children are taught to be open in their dealing with one another and with adults. They are encouraged to display affection openly and warmly towards each other.

It follows that anyone who asks children to be secretive will immediately cause alarm. As long as adults do not impose their fears about physical or mental abuse upon them, children are naturally open and honest and indeed find it very distressing to keep secrets, particularly from people about whom they care. Teachers, police, and adults must always be prepared to listen to a child who seems distressed.

The straightforward message is that children have the same rights that everyone else has. They have the right to protect their bodies, and they have the right to say, "No." Finally they have the right to be heard sympathetically when they are troubled or distressed.

An underrated and very prevalent abuse in schools is bullying. If children have experienced it, bullying saps their morale, spoils their concentration, and their work. Moreover, the quality of their lives suffers. Police can help kids to understand that they have a right to be safe and well. No one has a right to interfere with that right, and they should be encouraged to talk about any kind of bullying. Children who are taught to respect themselves and respect others are very likely to develop into healthy mature adults.

Children must be confident when they go to an adult to talk about a problem—abuse, bullying, or anything—that they will be listened to and believed. Many adults listen to young people but never hear them. Children very rarely lie about issues as private, difficult, and possibly traumatic as these. They need to know that if they find the courage to tell an adult about a problem, they will not face recriminations but find affection and support. Children can learn and understand how to deal with crime prevention as early as three years of age.

A CODE FOR PARENTS

Police can provide parents with some guidelines for the personal safety of their children. Certainly, parents need to know at all times where their children are. Children need to know where they may go and when they are expected home. Parents who are absent from their home should be careful about baby-sitters, especially sitters who are not well known to the family. A local baby-sitting support group might be a reassuring alternative to blindly hiring a sitter. Once the sitter has left the house, parents should get their child's reaction to the babysitter. Parents should make sure that adequate arrangements are made *everyday* for their children to get safely to and from school. Parents need to know about the lessons in personal safety that their children are learning at school in order to reinforce them at home. Parents should ensure that their child knows how to get help if necessary. Does the child know how to use a phone to dial 0 for operator and use the emergency 911 system?

PROTECTION FOR WOMEN

Police can provide a great deal of valid, sensible advice to help women avoid criminal attack and increase their sense of well-being and of safety from crime. One of the most prevalent problems for women is the violence directed against them in their homes.

DOMESTIC VIOLENCE

When police consider the amount of violence in homes, they are dealing with the unknown. Police researchers do not know the scale of the problems, although it may be considerable. They do not even know accurately where domestic violence is likely to occur, although research indicates that it is as prevalent in middle class suburbs as inner city districts.

Anyone who has ever been victimized understands the phrase, "living in fear." Domestic violence is the most confusing and cruel indignation any woman can suffer. A woman must often choose between her responsibility to hold her family together and the possibility of being mentally damaged, physically injured, or possibly murdered.

In 1984, the U.S. Attorney General's Task Force on Family Violence reported a sickening pattern of widespread spouse abuse, incest, child molestation, and abuse of children and elderly relatives. Regrettably, many police officers tend to dismiss family violence, because what occurs within a family home is, they believe, not their concern. A large number of homicides committed in the United States and Great Britain occur in domestic scenes. Many of them could have been prevented by firm police action. The Task Force made a number of recommendations that remain valid. It urged police agencies to adopt a policy on domestic violence. It suggested that the basic definition of violence committed by one spouse on another should be the same whether the offense takes place within a home or on a street. An offender should be arrested whenever sufficient evidence exists to justify proceedings. Officers should be informed about sources of support in cases of domestic violence, like crisis resolution centers and marital counsellors. Police should report their course of action in every domestic dispute. Dispatchers and patrol officers should treat these cases as the high priority incidents that they are.

More than most crimes, domestic violence is characterized by its repeated and sustained nature. It is not characterized by an occasional heated argument between domestic partners. Domestic violence concerns either outright violence or threats of violence. That kind of violence is police business, wherever it occurs. Many agencies have a domestic violence policy as a result of state legislation like, for example, the Illinois Domestic Violence Act. In cases of domestic violence, officers are compelled to make available to the injured party the option of initiating an assault complaint. They are always required to submit a report on the incident and are encouraged to use victim assistance groups within their local communities. Some departments may not have policies on domestic violence but in terms of problem-solving, the mental attitude of the responding officer is important in a violent situation. Do police simply calm an initial situation, answer another different call, and wait to be called back to the same initial situation the next night or following week? Or do police take a few minutes to try to discover the cause of violence? Maybe it is drug abuse, alcohol abuse, incompatibility, or a combination of causes. If police cannot do something about the cause of violence, they must ask themselves who can.

Domestic violence can be deterred, when law permits, by the immediate arrest of the abusing spouse. If an arrest can be made, it sends a clear message that violent behavior will not be tolerated and will be subject to legal sanction.

WOMEN AND CHILDREN
Key Points

Children

Remember referrals to outside agencies like:

state child protection agencies.

Catholic social services.

city hospitals.

abuse-counseling programs.

city social service programs.

Children are entitled to personal respect and privacy.

Children should be discouraged from keeping secrets from their parents and teachers.

Never forget that most children will never be abused.

Never portray adults as threats; be positive and indicate to them which adults can provide help.

Remember that much abuse is interfamilial, but do not forget about "Stranger-Danger."

Remind parents that they should know where their children are at all times.

9

Police Evaluations of Crime Prevention

Within the context of history, policing as a specialized profession is relatively new. People once policed their communities themselves, but as the Industrial Revolution lured more people into cities, the task of maintaining public order became more than volunteer patrols could do.

Until the advent of modern technology, police officers were members of the communities they served. A foot patrol officer on a permanent beat knew who to trust and who to mistrust. His intimate knowledge of the dynamics of the neighborhood allowed him to tailor his responses to the community's needs and priorities.

In modern cities, however, the role of the police shifted from peacekeeper to crime-fighter. The aloof, serious Sergeant Joe Friday of "Dragnet" who wanted "just the facts" replaced the friendly officer in Norman Rockwell's painting who gives a lost child an ice cream cone.

Future police officers will need the freedom and autonomy to expand their traditional jobs by balancing reactive efforts with proactive initiatives aimed at reducing and controlling contemporary crime and drug problems. These community officers will discover that they must become community problem-solvers.

The police in the United States and in the United Kingdom are working toward the prevention of crime. Community involvement is crucial to police work in both countries.

As new programs evolve, the need to evaluate police success becomes vital. What works and what does not work become the criteria for organizational development. Overcoming the limitations to police productivity, administrators are prime users of productivity improvement programs and measures. As a means for managerial control, productivity measures, however, often fail to provide police administrators with an appraisal of organizational policies and organizational effectiveness. Indeed, the measures frequently used by police agencies leave much to be desired as tools of operational analysis. Consequently, the selection of operationally relevant productivity measures is a difficult and crucial challenge to the police administrator.

MEASURING PRODUCTION

When activities are routine and repetitive, production records can be analyzed to gauge productivity and to provide a data base for managerial decision-making. Filing, typing, and fingerprinting operations are functions that are amenable to this type of evaluation. The number of information cards filed or the number of pages typed or filed provide a basis for measuring and comparing employee output. Combined with time and motion studies, such output measures help establish standards of work performance for specific duties.

Production records provide a rather uncomplicated way to evaluate the performance of a unit. Production measurement systems, however, have disadvantages. The impersonal statistical report is often unpopular with employees. Morale drops, particularly if employees perceive that the reports generate work "speed ups." Production measurement systems are also costly in terms of data collection and data analysis time. Costs in time and morale might conceivably outweigh the benefits of a particular production measurement program.

Production records alone never show an employee's true worth to an organization. Consequently, production records should always be considered in conjunction with other measures or contributions by employees or work groups. If a multiple measures approach is not used, extreme caution should be taken in applying production records as the standard against which the efficiency and effectiveness of employees or organizational units are measured. The injudicious overemphasis on production measures by police managers can severely compromise positive goal-oriented approaches to law enforcement. Instead, employees become self-focused manipulators of production statistics.

Production measures often present distorted evaluations of organizational performance for another reason. A variety of environments surround police departments, and raw measures of output cannot be understood apart from the political culture and community norms that help define acceptable levels of police output.

PER CAPITA COSTS OF POLICE SERVICES

The cost of police services per capita is a frequently used productivity measurement. The measure is easily derived (police budget divided by jurisdictional population) and permits comparisons over time and across jurisdictions. The measure is extremely flexible and may be employed by different people to condemn a police department or to exalt its efficiency.

One interpretation of the per capita measure is that if the per capita expenditure for police service in City A is high relative to other jurisdictions, then City A's police services are inefficient or ineffective. Before such a conclusion is justified, however, one must know more about the compared services.

Two cities of approximately the same geographical size and population may have widely different per capita costs, because the functions of one police department include activities not demanded by the citizenry of the other. For example, the police department in City A may require an intelligence division; the police department in City B may not need one or have one.

Considerations of political culture can also reduce the utility of comparing per capita costs among police departments in different jurisdictions. Under a local policy of minimal regulation dictated by private interests and the local government policymakers, per capita police costs in City A may be quite low. In the more service-oriented political culture of City B, per capita police costs may be quite high. The fact that City A's minimalist enforcement policies might compound long-term crime costs simply underscores the limitations of per capita costs as a productivity measure.

CRIME RATES AS MEASURES OF PRODUCTIVITY

The basic police mission is to prevent crime and disorder. However, the police are not solely accountable for crime increases or decreases. Many agencies and individuals in the community dedicate themselves to the prevention of crime and delinquency. They include the sheriff's department, the prosecuting attorney, judges, court personnel, probation and parole officers, reform schools, prisons, jails, social welfare agencies, the school system, and the family.

With such an undeniably complex dispersion of responsibility, using crime rates as the measure of police efficiency is not scientifically acceptable. Because many factors affect the incidence of crime, the police can only share the credit for crime reduction or for crime increases.

The Uniform Crime Reporting Committee noted what happens when crime rates become proxies for police productivity:

...another difficulty...which partially explains the reluctance of some police forces to compile and publish reports showing the number of crimes committed. . .is derived from the tendency to charge the crime rate against the police rather than against the community, and (from) the temptation to draw from such statistics broad generalizations concerning the relative efficiency of various police forces.

Two general conclusions about the use of crime rates to measure police effectiveness seem warranted. First, statistics showing the volume of crime do not provide a sufficient measure of police efficiency or effectiveness. Second, even when such statistics are uniformly compiled across jurisdictions, as they are in England, comparisons among jurisdictions do not establish a valid "effectiveness ranking" of the compared departments.

This second conclusion is not only a matter of methodology but also a matter of local conventions regarding acceptable levels of crime. No consensus exists regarding what constitutes low, medium, or high levels of crime. To establish such standards would require the accurate measurement of public tolerance, and this measurement varies from region to region and from community to community. Even within a community, developing crime reduction goals can be difficult. Should crime be eliminated or reduced to a reasonable level? If so, what is meant by reasonable?

CASES CLEARED BY ARRESTS

In contrast to the crime rate, the percentage of cases cleared by arrest appears to be a more discriminating barometer of police efficiency than crime rates. A police department can end a one-person crime wave by arresting a robber who is linked to several dozen offenses. Nonetheless, the case clearance rate also presents problems as an absolute and relative measure of police efficiency.

As a relative measure of police department productivity, case clearances confront many of the problems that weaken per capita costs and crime rates as productivity measures. Enforcement policies vary from city to city. When municipal, county, state, and federal law enforcement jurisdictions overlap, case clearances may be double-counted, or the apprehending agency may not get credit for arresting an offender.

When police administrators, local legislators, city managers, and mayors shape jurisdiction-specific enforcement policies, the result may be a policy conducive to high case clearances (no vice or illegal use of intoxicants in one town) or a policy resulting in a lower level of case clearances (the tolerance of vice in a district for tourists). When the case clearance rate is so fundamentally determined by such policies, as is often the case, little information of value is gained by evaluating police efficiency and effectiveness on the basis of case clearance rates.

PERCENTAGE OF CONVICTIONS OBTAINED

The percentage of convictions obtained in police cases is used as a measure of police efficiency in the investigation of crimes, the marshalling of evidence, and the presentation of court testimony.

As with the measures discussed, the percentage of convictions cannot and does not stand in a one-to-one relationship with police effectiveness and police productivity. The conviction rate is a function of the quality of the county or city attorney's staff, the prosecutor's policy about pursuing cases in which convictions are less than certain, and the skill of local defense attorneys. Other factors that complicate the relationship between police activity and the conviction rate include a general bias in the juror pool for or against certain classes of offenses, and the balance the judiciary strikes between the investigatory latitude of police and the constitutional protection of defendants.

The conviction rate reveals more about prosecutorial and judicial effectiveness than about police effectiveness. In general, the assembly line method of administering justice warrants careful review to identify malfunctioning operations. Most jurisdictions could profit from closer police and prosecutorial coordination during arraignment in order to identify cases that require special pre-trial work.

VALID MEASUREMENTS FOR CRIME PREVENTION

Statistics are flexible numbers. A single set of statistics can produce multiple images of a single phenomenon and can even support contradictory hypotheses. A police chief, addressing a local civic organization, may only mention statistics that make the department and the chief look good. The chief will ignore data that indicate ineffective police work. Statistics presented in a self-aggrandizing manner rarely stand as valid standards of productivity measurement. Unfortunately, the self-serving statistical compilation is all too frequent in police work and in other areas of public administration.

Most data pertaining to police activity are easily distorted—the police can be made to look good or bad. Even when the data are carefully compiled and show what they purport to show—conviction rates, case clearance rates, or per capita police expenditures—the data do not represent a direct measure of police productivity. None of these measures successfully isolates the impact of police activity from the effects of other agencies in the criminal justice system, in government, and in the community at large.

All of these measures have an overly ambitious frame of reference. When second, third, and fourth order results of police activity—case clearances, convictions, per capita costs—are the frame of reference for productivity measurement, police are faced with a mammoth and perhaps impossible analytical task. To do the job right, police must determine multifactorial relationships among activities, community standards, political culture, numerous public and private agencies, budget allocations, crime rates, case clearances, and convictions. Even if police were able to do this, they might find comparatively high crime rates associated with police activity that measure up to accepted professional standards in every respect.

To gauge police productivity, a standard of measurement is needed that focuses on police work. The frame of reference should be day-to-day police activity. Observation of specific officers in specific communities should be utilized as a measure of the immediate and direct impact of police activity on the incidence of crime.

The heart of police work is presence in the community, and presence indicates patrol and field contacts. The field contact, in particular, is an activity which results in direct and immediate effects. The crime consequences—spot-prevention, short-term diminishment, or displacement—are primarily a function of police activity in the field.

Field contacts are activities that permit the direct measurement of police productivity. To establish a relationship between field activity and crime prevention goals, it is necessary to have a formal process of setting goals within the organization.

SETTING GOALS

Establishing goals for a municipal police organization is the crucial first step in productivity measurement. Before setting operational goals, an overall mission statement is important. The mission statement establishes the direction for the police organization. Then the organization must identify community conditions that are most affected by police activity. Although the police are responsible for guarding against a wide array of crimes, some crimes increase or decrease in response to police activity more than others.

If one were to select a crime and track its incidence over time in a particular area in order to gauge the effectiveness of a series of patrol strategies, a repressible crime such as burglary, robbery, or auto theft would be preferable to an eruptive crime like domestic violence. Repressible crimes simply have a more direct relationship to police activity than do eruptive crimes.

Police officers should always evaluate, in their own minds or in written reports to their superiors, how successful or how unsuccessful their crime prevention efforts have been within their precincts. What has worked? How has it worked? Why has it worked? More importantly perhaps, what has failed?

10

Future Changes for Police and Communities

From suspect behavior to victim vulnerability, this book has been written in a format for crime prevention. The ideas and suggestions outlined in the text are designed to prevent crime.

Crime will not be reduced in a city or neighborhood by the police. Crime will be reduced when the police and people work together to prevent crime.

The FBI Uniform Crime Reports give a description of "crime factors" each year which reveal an interesting picture of accountability for crime. Of the numerous factors mentioned, it is obvious that many are not subject to the control or influence of the police. The quality of education in a community and the community's recreational opportunities directly affect crime trends, but the line-item budgets of police organizations do not include funds to improve schools or recreational facilities.

The Uniform Crime Report states that people between the ages of fifteen years and twenty years are responsible for almost 50 percent of serious crime. If a community has a large population in this age group, it is somewhat predictable that crime data will be influenced by these simple demographics.

The police should be accountable for coordinating community efforts in crime prevention. The police cannot be accountable for all the causes of crime. According to the "General Principles of Organization" outlined in *Municipal Police Administration* by O.W. Wilson in 1961, lines of authority and responsibility should be made as definite and direct as possible. Responsibility cannot be placed without delegating commensurate authority, and authority should not be delegated without holding the user to account for the use he makes of it.

These basic police management principles directly relate to the problem of the police assuming responsibility for crime while having little or no authority over its causes. This dichotomy causes problems for the police. Given all the factors that have a direct impact on crime but that are not under the authority of police, one can see that those factors are in direct violation of the principles outlined by O.W. Wilson.

The purpose of emphasizing this conflict in principles is to demonstrate that adherence to outdated management dictums has limited application in police theory and organization. America's police administrators, for all practical purposes, adhere to military management and leadership principles. Continued adherence to these principles is making it difficult for police organizations to adopt new ways of conducting police business. Crime prevention should contribute to changes by directing police effort at prevention rather than toward reaction.

Crime is a community problem. Its causes are created by community issues and community failures—not just police issues and police failures.

Crime prevention requires community involvement and community accountability. Albert Einstein stated:

> It is the duty of every man of good will to strive steadfastly in his own little world to do what is right...If he makes an honest attempt in this direction without being crushed and trampled under foot by his contemporaries, he may consider himself and the community to which he belongs lucky.

The police with community involvement can prevent crime.

Index

alarms, 13, 25, 27, 39-41, 53-5, 60
  "bells-only" system, 53-4
  remote signaling system, 54
arrests, 84
armed robbery, 39
arson, 37, 42-3, 46

Bottoms, Anthony, 13
British Crime Survey (1983), 21
British Metropolitan Police, 12
bullying, 73-4

burglary, 7, 12-3, 15, 17, 21, 32, 37,
  40-1, 47-8, 50-5, 57, 62, 88
businesses, 4, 17, 37-46, 64, 67

cars, 4, 12, 17, 20-30, 39, 42, 57, 62
children, 9-10, 13, 15, 57, 61, 65, 67,
  71-4, 78
closed-circuit television, 24, 40, 43
"Communities in Schools," 67
community policing, 3-4, 10, 13-4,
  16, 18, 29, 31, 34, 44, 64-6, 80,
  83, 90-1

93